The Calm Within

A Stoic Reset to Reclaim
Your Inner Power

The Calm Within

A Stoic Reset to Reclaim
Your Inner Power

Rodolfo Costa

Copyright © 2025 Rodolfo Costa

All rights reserved. This book is protected under international copyright laws and treaties.

No part of this book may be reproduced, stored in a retrieval system, or transmitted in any form or by any means—electronic, mechanical, photocopying, recording, or otherwise—without the prior written permission of the author.

The Calm Within: A Stoic Reset to Reclaim Your Inner Power
ISBN: 979-8-9936270-0-7
RC Independently Published

Disclaimer

The information, exercises, and prompts in this book are provided for educational, inspirational, and entertainment purposes only. They are not intended as a substitute for professional advice, therapy, medical treatment, or legal counsel. The author and publisher do not render legal, psychological, medical, or other professional services.

Readers are encouraged to consult qualified professionals—such as licensed therapists, medical practitioners, or legal advisors—regarding their individual circumstances and needs. The author and publisher disclaim responsibility for any actions, decisions, or outcomes arising from the use of this book.

The practices and exercises described herein may not be suitable for everyone. Readers should consider their own limitations, preferences, and physical or mental health conditions before engaging in any suggested activities.

References to external resources, websites, or products do not constitute endorsement. The author and publisher are not responsible for the content, reliability, or availability of third-party resources, nor for any issues that may arise from their use.

By reading and applying this book, you acknowledge and agree that you assume full responsibility for your actions, choices, and interpretations. The author and publisher expressly disclaim liability for any damages, injuries, or losses that may result.

Dedication

To every reader who opens these pages: may you find not escape, but a compass—one that points you back to calm, to courage, and to the quiet strength already within you. This book is also for those who seek strength rather than ease, who choose calm in the storm, and who remember that the compass is always within.

Table of Contents

Introduction 1
- Why a Stoic Reset Matters Today 1
- The Noise of Modern Life: Speed, Pressure, and Endless Distraction 2
- Timeless Wisdom: Stoicism's Relevance in a Restless Age 3
- Practical, Not Academic: A Philosophy for Real People 5
- A Reset Program: How to Use This Book as a Lifelong Rhythm 6
- An Invitation 8

Reset 1: The Still Point in a Turning World 9
- Two Mornings: chaos vs. clarity (a parable) 9
- The Search for Inner Calm 10
- Marcus Aurelius on Stillness 11
- Resetting the Mind in a Chaotic Culture 11
- Practical Resets for Modern Life 12
- Reset in Action 13
- Reflection Questions 14
- Reset 1 Takeaway 14

Reset 2: Train Your Inner Voice 17
- The Quiet War (a parable) 17
- Thoughts as Seeds of Action 18

- Negative Spirals vs. Deliberate Thought 19
- Modern Echoes of the Stoic Lesson 20
- Training the Inner Voice. 20
- Reset in Action 22
- Reflection Questions 23
- Reset 2 Takeaway 23

Reset 3: Focus on What is Yours. 25
- Storm, Soft Opening (a parable) 25
- The Stoic Dichotomy of Control. 26
- Why This Is So Hard Today 27
- Freedom Through Choosing What's Truly Ours . . . 29
- Practical Exercises for Focus 30
- Reset in Action 31
- Pause and Reflect 31
- Reset 3 Takeaway 32

Reset 4: Reframe the World Around You 33
- The Cracked Window (a parable). 33
- Epictetus on Perspective 34
- The Present as Training Ground 35
- Reset in Action 39
- Reflection Questions 40
- Reset 4 Takeaway 40

Reset 5: Anchor Yourself in Values 43
- The Promise and the Ping (a parable). 43

- Virtue as the Stoics' Highest Good 44
- The Four Virtues, Translated................... 45
- Building a Personal Compass 47
- The Challenge of Noise and Pressure 49
- Reset in Action 50
- Reflection Questions 51
- Reset 5 Takeaway 51

Reset 6: Choose Growth Over Comfort 53

- The Broken Elevator (a parable) 53
- Seneca on Voluntary Hardship 54
- Why Growth and Comfort Rarely Coexist 55
- Practices for Resilience........................ 57
- Stoic Voices on Hardship 59
- Reset in Action 60
- Reflection Questions 60
- Reset 6 Takeaway 61

Reset 7: Release What Weighs You Down 63

- The Stone in the Pack (a parable) 63
- Chains of Yesterday: Grudges, Envy, Comparison, Anger 64
- Forgiveness as Strength 65
- Boundaries With Compassion 66
- Reset in Action 69
- Reflection Questions 69
- Reset 7 Takeaway 70

Reset 8: Build Daily Rituals for Calm.......... 71
- The Three Bells (a parable)..................... 71
- Why Rhythm Matters......................... 72
- Journaling as a Stoic Tool 75
- Living Wisdom as Rhythm, Not Theory.......... 76
- Reset in Action 78
- Reflection Questions 78
- Reset 8 Takeaway 79

Reset 9: Strength Through Connection 81
- The Bridge on Maple Street (a parable)........... 81
- Stoicism Is Not Isolation — It's Service 82
- Marcus Aurelius: The Hive and the Bee 83
- Relationships, Community, and Empathy Today... 84
- Community in Practice........................ 85
- Practical Exercises for Connection 87
- Reset in Action 88
- Reflection Questions 89
- Reset 9 Takeaway 89

Reset 10: Face the Future with Courage 91
- The Lantern in the Fog (a parable) 91
- Uncertainty and Change as Constants 92
- The Mind's Bad Deals with the Future 93
- Memento Mori: Preparing for Adversity and Mortality 95
- Practical Exercises for Courage................. 99

- Reset in Action 100
- Reflection Questions 100
- Reset 10 Takeaway 101

Epilogue: The Calm Within You 103

- The Pocket Compass (a parable) 103
- A Reset as an Ongoing Journey 104
- Why Small, Consistent Actions Shape Character 105
- Calm and the Virtues Revisited 106
- The Compass as Lifelong Practice 107
- An Invitation to Live Steady, Calm, and Unshaken 108

Request for a Review 111

About the Author 113

Introduction

"You have power over your mind—not outside events. Realize this, and you will find strength." — Marcus Aurelius

Why a Stoic Reset Matters Today

You wake before you are ready. The glow of the screen greets you before the light of the day does. Messages, headlines, reminders, and demands stack up like bricks before your eyes are fully open. Coffee tastes less like comfort and more like fuel for a race you didn't sign up for. By the time you reach your desk, you've already compared your life to strangers, rehearsed conversations that may never happen, and surrendered chunks of attention to forces outside your control.

It is not that any one of these things is unbearable. It is the layering: speed over pressure over distraction until the day feels like a moving walkway that you cannot step off. By noon, your attention is confetti. By night, you are weary in a way that sleep doesn't cure.

Calm feels like a luxury—something reserved for weekends that actually stay free, or vacations where you can finally hear yourself think. It's easy to imagine that peace exists somewhere else: on a mountain, at a retreat, or in a life simpler than your own. But waiting for life to grant you calm is like waiting for the sea to stop moving before you row.

This book is about another way. A Stoic reset is not an escape from life's turbulence but a deliberate return to what is always within your reach: your perspective, your choices, your character. It is a way of stopping mid-current, taking a breath, and setting your oars back in the direction that matters most. You don't need perfect conditions. You need the skill of returning.

The Noise of Modern Life: Speed, Pressure, and Endless Distraction

Modern life is abundant in convenience and impoverished in clarity. We live with miracles in our pockets: messages that travel continents in seconds, access to libraries larger than empires, and tools that automate what used to consume entire days. Yet, with these miracles comes a steady erosion of attention.

Speed is the first culprit. Every new tool promises to save time, but the time saved is quickly filled with more obligations. We move faster and faster without ever feeling finished. Urgency becomes the default mood.

Pressure follows. Metrics stalk our days—likes, steps, sales, unread counts. Numbers meant to guide us become numbers that define us. The self turns into a cockpit of blinking dials: always monitoring, rarely present.

Finally, distraction. Notifications chirp like small emergencies, shattering focus into fragments too thin to hold anything meaningful. Our minds learn to skim instead of dwell, to react instead of reflect. The cost is subtle but corrosive: restlessness that shapes not only our days but our character.

And yet, the world has always had storms. In the time of Marcus Aurelius, the storms were arrogance, politics, betrayal, and war. In ours, they are inboxes that refill endlessly, a culture of comparison, and a low hum of anxiety that never switches off. The challenge is not new. Only the form has changed.

The Stoics understood: we cannot demand calm conditions. We must build calmer crafts.

Timeless Wisdom: Stoicism's Relevance in a Restless Age

Stoicism was not born in libraries or ivory towers. It was tested in marketplaces, council chambers, battlefields, and households. It was practiced by people trying to live decently in worlds as messy and unpredictable as ours.

Marcus Aurelius wrote his *Meditations* in a war tent, reminding himself to be just and steady when surrounded by ambition and fear. Epictetus, once enslaved, discovered that while others could control his body, no one could control his judgment without his consent. Seneca, advisor to emperors, wrote letters on grief, wealth, and resilience while navigating a court thick with corruption and danger.

Their world was not calm. Neither is ours. But their insights endure because they refuse to depend on conditions. At the core lies a distinction so clear it changes everything:

- Some things are within your control: your judgments, your choices, your actions right now.

- Some things are not: other people's opinions, the final outcomes of complex situations, the weather, the past.

Confusing the two leads to suffering. Sorting them leads to freedom.

From this foundation flows a posture fit for any century:

- **Guard your mind.** Thoughts arrive uninvited, but you choose which ones earn your assent.

- **Do the good in front of you.** You cannot fix the whole world, but you can act with fairness, courage, and clarity in the moment at hand.

- **Widen your view.** Zooming out restores proportion; insults shrink, priorities sharpen.

- **Remember mortality.** Life is finite. That truth doesn't paralyze; it energizes.

This wisdom does not rely on sandals or scrolls. It works in sneakers and spreadsheets. It works for parents, leaders, students, and anyone trying to live with steadiness in a world that profits from distraction.

Practical, Not Academic: A Philosophy for Real People

If the word "philosophy" conjures images of lectures or jargon, set them aside. Stoicism was never meant to be a classroom exercise. It was meant to be lived.

That is why this book is not an academic treatise but a handbook. It will not ask you to memorize obscure vocabulary or track historical footnotes. It will ask you to try small practices in the thick of ordinary life.

When your email pings, when your child cries, when your coworker snaps, when you find yourself doomscrolling at midnight—these are the moments where philosophy lives or dies. A Stoic reset is not about retreating from life but about returning to it with steadiness, clarity, and calm.

The aim here is modest but powerful: to help you make better decisions under pressure, to free you from habits of rumination, to steady your presence so that people experience you as clear, kind, and unshaken.

This book is light on abstraction and heavy on use. Each chapter offers:

- **A parable.** Because stories carry truths better than instructions.

- **A Stoic frame.** Ancient principles explained plainly, without ornament.

- **Modern friction points.** Where this principle is tested today—notifications, deadlines, comparison culture.

- **Practical resets.** Repeatable actions, some quick, some deeper, to re-center yourself.

- **Reflections.** Questions or lines to carry with you.

The goal is not for you to nod along but for your week to feel different. More deliberate. Less brittle. More yours.

A Reset Program: How to Use This Book as a Lifelong Rhythm

This book offers ten resets. They are not sequential steps to finish once, but rhythms to return to—like tuning an instrument.

Some days you will drift. Some days you will forget. That does not erase the practice. Every return is progress.

Introduction

The resets include:

1. Finding stillness in a turning world.
2. Training your inner voice.
3. Reclaiming focus by distinguishing what is yours to control.
4. Reframing hardships through perspective.
5. Anchoring in values that outlast noise.
6. Choosing growth over comfort.
7. Releasing what weighs you down.
8. Building daily rituals for calm.
9. Strengthening yourself through connection.
10. Facing the future with courage.

Each reset will meet you with a parable, a Stoic foundation, practices to try, and reflection questions to personalize.

You are not expected to master all at once. Begin where your need is loudest. Practice until it feels like habit. Add another. The aim is not to graduate but to deepen—like the wheelwright who never makes a perfect wheel, but learns to shape better ones more quickly, with less wasted effort.

Think of these resets as a compass. Not a map that claims to predict every turn, but a tool that points you back to your true north whenever you drift.

An Invitation

This book is not promising you a life free of storms. It is promising you the skills to row through them with clarity and calm.

The invitation is simple:

- Live steady. Lower your center of gravity with simple practices that hold you upright.

- Live calmly. Not as indifference, but as the refusal to be driven by your first impulse.

- Live unshaken. Not because nothing touches you, but because what touches you meets someone with a spine.

You do not control the waters. You do not control the weather. But you can row—deliberately, courageously, calmly. Again and again. That is enough.

Reset 1

The Still Point in a Turning World

Finding calm at the center of chaos

Two Mornings: chaos vs. clarity (a parable)

Rush hour in the city. Cars inch forward, horns echo between glass towers, and crowds hurry across sidewalks, faces lit by glowing screens. Somewhere in that swarm, a young professional clutches her coffee—already late, already anxious. Her mind races between unfinished emails, the memory of a tense conversation waiting to resume, and a news alert that made her stomach sink.

She tells herself: *If I could just catch up—if I could get ahead—I'd finally feel calm.*

But the faster she runs, the further peace drifts away. Every step forward feels like running on a treadmill—sweat without progress, motion without rest.

Now shift scenes. Two thousand years earlier, another morning begins. The Roman emperor Marcus Aurelius rises before dawn. He doesn't reach for a device or dictate orders. He opens a worn journal and writes to himself:

"People look for retreats for themselves, in the country, by the sea, or in the hills. You too are very much in the habit of yearning for these same things. But this is altogether unphilosophical, when it is open to you, at any time you want, to retreat into yourself." - *Meditations*

One morning begins in noise. The other begins in clarity. The difference lies in the reset.

The Search for Inner Calm

Modern life rarely allows pause. We wake to alarms, scroll through headlines we can't control, and rush into tasks before our minds have even caught up. By mid-morning, we're already swept away by demands.

We tell ourselves that calm will come once the world slows down—when the inbox is clear, the errands are finished, the bills paid. But the Stoics remind us: waiting for a quieter world is like waiting for the ocean to stop moving. Calm is not something you receive from circumstances; it is something you cultivate in spite of them.

Seneca wrote that tranquility of mind is the reward of living with reason, not of controlling fortune. Epictetus reminded his students that people are disturbed not by events, but by their judgments of them. Marcus compared the soul to a rock: steady no matter what waves strike against it.

The common thread is this: storms will always come, but calm is always possible.

Marcus Aurelius on Stillness

No Stoic embodied the pursuit of inner calm more than Marcus Aurelius. He was emperor, commander, father, philosopher—millions depended on his decisions. He endured invasions, plagues, and court intrigues that would have broken lesser men. And yet, in his private notes, he returned again and again to the practice of stillness.

He reminded himself that peace is not found by fleeing to the mountains but by retreating inward. Even in a palace, surrounded by advisers and soldiers, he could pause, breathe, and return to what mattered most: reason, justice, and virtue.

If Marcus Aurelius could find stillness while ruling an empire, then we can find it while waiting in traffic, standing in line, or navigating a stressful meeting. His lesson is clear: circumstances are never calm. People rarely behave as we wish. Yet stillness is always available as a practice.

Resetting the Mind in a Chaotic Culture

If Rome was noisy, our age is relentless. The Stoics did not face smartphones, but they faced gossip, political strife, and constant unrest. Our distractions simply glow brighter.

Technology compresses time. What once took days now takes seconds. But instead of giving us peace, it delivers endless urgency. News updates arrive by the hour. Messages demand instant replies. Social media invites comparison on repeat. No wonder our minds feel fractured.

Home is not immune. Parents rush from work to after-school pickups, juggle dinner, homework, bills, and the invisible weight of keeping everyone moving. Even in our most private spaces, the churn continues. Silence is rare. Stillness rarer.

The Stoics remind us: calm doesn't depend on a quieter world—it depends on resetting our response. We cannot slow the storm, but we can drop anchor.

Practical Resets for Modern Life

- **The Digital Pause** – Before opening an app, ask: *Am I choosing this, or reacting?* That pause restores control.

- **The Evening Reflection** – Each night, jot down two or three lines: Where did I lose calm today? How will I respond differently tomorrow? Patterns emerge over time.

- **Reframing Chaos** – Treat distractions as training. Each interruption is a chance to practice patience instead of reaction.

- **The Breath Ritual** – Set a reminder three times a day. Stop, close your eyes, breathe deeply five times. Anchor your body so your mind follows.

- **The Physical Reset** – Change your environment for two minutes: step outside, stretch, walk down the hall. The shift signals your nervous system to settle.

- **The "Not Yet" Rule** – When impulse urges you to respond, post, or buy instantly, whisper *not yet*. Delay often reveals what is unnecessary.

- **The Small Retreat** – Once a week, take 15 minutes to sit without phone, book, or noise. Just breathe and notice. It is training for presence.

Calm is not found in extraordinary escapes but in ordinary moments repeated with care.

Reset in Action

Return to the young professional in the city. She cannot erase traffic or silence her phone. But she can reset.

At red lights, she pauses and breathes.

Before her meeting, she reminds herself: *I will show up with calm. That is mine to control.*

At night, she opens her journal and writes a single line: *Today I returned to myself.*

The world did not change. She did. And in that change, she discovered calm.

Reflection Questions

- Where do I most often lose my calm—at work, at home, or online?//
- What small retreat could I practice daily to return to my still point?
- How might my relationships shift if I brought stillness instead of stress?
- What is one situation this week where I could practice calm as a discipline, not wait for calm as a mood?

Reset 1 Takeaway

Stillness is not passivity. It is power.

The Stoics remind us that calm is not found by fleeing the world, but by standing unshaken within it. Marcus Aurelius could find it while ruling an empire; you can find it while running a meeting, waiting in line, or sitting in traffic.

The storm will always swirl. Demands will always come. But stillness is the citadel of the soul—a place you can carry anywhere.

The Still Point in a Turning World

When the world rushes, slow down.
When the noise grows, pause.
When the sea rages, drop anchor.

This is your first reset: to rediscover the still point in a turning world—not as escape, but as discipline.

A quiet center steadies you in chaos. But steadiness of thought is only the beginning. You must also train the voice that speaks within. That is the next reset: shaping your inner voice into an ally, not an enemy.

Reset 2

Train Your Inner Voice

Your inner voice is not background noise—it's the script of your life.

The Quiet War (a parable)

A designer stared at the blank canvas glowing on her screen. The deadline loomed, but the real battle wasn't on the page. Inside, her mind fired sharp arrows: *You're not ready. They'll see through you. Why even try?*

Her shoulders tightened. She thought about shutting the laptop, checking messages, distracting herself. Then she paused. She named the storm: *fear.* Instead of running, she argued back—with evidence. Three past projects had been praised. Two clients had sent thank-you notes. One colleague had asked her advice just last week. She set a twenty-minute timer.

By the bell, the canvas wasn't finished—but it wasn't empty either. The storm hadn't vanished. But it had orders.

The Stoics called this the inner contest: the battle not against armies or weather, but against the untrained voice that rises inside each of us. Victory doesn't come by silencing it. Victory comes by training it.

Thoughts as Seeds of Action

The Stoics noticed what modern psychology later confirmed: thoughts don't stop at the mind's door. They spill into words, choices, and habits until they shape the person you become.

- **Impressions arrive uninvited.** The Stoics used the word *phantasia*—raw impressions, flashes of emotion, images of gain or loss, often misleading.

- **Assent is your choice.** Epictetus drilled this point: you cannot stop impressions, but you can decide whether to agree with them. Assent is the hinge.

- **Thoughts become posture → words → habits → character.** Every repeated assent writes another line in the script of your life.

Seneca compared the mind to a field: if you neglect it, weeds of panic and envy grow fast. But if you plant carefully and tend with discipline, it yields calm, courage, and wisdom.

Marcus Aurelius sharpened the same point in his *Meditations*: "Such as are your habitual thoughts, such also will be the character of your mind; for the soul is dyed by the thoughts." The dye takes with repetition.

Negative Spirals vs. Deliberate Thought

Most of us know the spiral:

- One mistake → "I always fail."

- One rejection → "I'm never good enough."

- One setback → "It's ruined forever."

This script becomes a loop. The more you rehearse it, the more convincing it sounds. The Stoics called these exaggerations "judgments" more dangerous than the events themselves. The fall may bruise; the judgment declares it fatal.

The alternative is not denial, but deliberate thought. To pause and name the storm. To question its exaggeration. To insert a more accurate line in the script:

- "This mistake is one data point, not my destiny."

- "That rejection hurts, but it doesn't define my worth."

- "This setback delays me; it doesn't destroy me."

Deliberate thought doesn't mean forced cheerfulness. It means refusing to hand the pen to panic.

Modern Echoes of the Stoic Lesson

The ancient arena was the Forum, the battlefield, the Senate. Ours is the inbox, the scroll, the meeting. But the voice is the same.

- **At work.** You misspeak in a meeting, and the inner voice plays it on loop: *They think you're incompetent.* But deliberate thought reframes: *I stumbled, but I contributed. One comment won't erase years of work.*

- **Online.** A post you wrote gets fewer likes than expected. The voice says: *You're invisible. You don't matter.* Stoic training answers: *Approval online is not my measure. What matters is whether I wrote with truth and fairness.*

- **In relationships.** A friend delays replying. The voice hisses: *They don't value you.* Stoic training asks: *Is this fact or assumption? Might they be busy, tired, or hurting?*

Each scene reveals the same fork: assent blindly and spiral, or pause and choose a steadier script.

Training the Inner Voice

Epictetus gave his students drills, not theories. So let's make this reset practical.

1. Guard the Gate

Imagine a guard at the door of your mind. Each thought knocks. You decide whether it enters. Ask three questions before granting entry:

- Is it true?
- Is it useful?
- Does it serve the person I want to become?

If not, don't let it in. Or let it in only as something to question, not to obey.

2. Rehearse Clean Lines

Write down a few short sentences to use when the storm rises. Examples:

- "This is just an impression, not a fact."
- "I can choose my response."
- "What virtue does this moment call for?"

Repeat them often. The dye of thought sets with practice.

3. The Thought Journal

Each evening, write down one spiral thought that struck you. Then rewrite it as a deliberate thought. Over time, the rewrites become faster, almost automatic.

4. The Twenty-Minute Test

When paralyzed by doubt, set a timer for twenty minutes. Do the task imperfectly. Often the storm shrinks once action begins. As Seneca said: "We suffer more in imagination than in reality."

5. Call and Response with a Stoic Voice

When your mind whispers, *I can't endure this,* answer with Marcus Aurelius: *"Nothing happens to anyone that he is not fitted by Nature to bear."*

When it protests, *This isn't fair,* remind yourself with his counsel: *"Waste no more time arguing about what a good man should be. Be one."*

The Stoics strengthened their inner dialogue by borrowing the words of their teachers until those truths became their own. You can do the same.

Reset in Action

Return to the designer with her blank canvas. Fear still knocked, but she trained her inner voice to answer differently: *I've done good work before. I can start small. Twenty minutes is mine to give.*

By the end of the week, the project wasn't flawless—but it was finished. Her storm had not disappeared. It had been ordered.

This is what training looks like: not silencing doubt forever, but teaching it to take its place.

Reflection Questions

- What phrases or judgments do I hear most often from my inner critic?

- Which of them are impressions—not facts—that I can choose not to assent to?

- What deliberate lines could I rehearse this week to train my voice?

- How might my character shift if I dyed my thoughts daily with courage, fairness, or patience?

Reset 2 Takeaway

Your inner voice is not background noise—it is the architect of your life. Left untrained, it builds spirals of panic, envy, and despair. Trained with patience, it builds courage, fairness, and calm.

The Stoics never denied the power of thought. They acknowledged it fully and insisted that mastery begins there. Marcus Aurelius dyed his soul with chosen thoughts. Epictetus drilled assent as the hinge of freedom. Seneca warned of suffering more in imagination than in reality.

This is your second reset: to train your inner voice. Guard the gate. Rehearse clean lines. Rewrite spirals. Act, however small, against the storm. Over time, your voice will stop sabotaging you and start serving you.

Not silence, but order. Not perfection, but progress. That is the sound of a life reclaimed.

But a trained voice alone cannot secure your calm. You must also learn to focus on what truly belongs to you, and release what never did. That is the next reset: mastering the Stoic discipline of control.

Reset 3

Focus on What is Yours

The freedom of letting go of what you don't control

Storm, Soft Opening (a parable)

The café had been ready for weeks—new cups stacked, plants just watered, a chalkboard sign reading *soft opening, be gentle*. At 6:57 a.m., the owner stood behind the counter, her feet bouncing on the floor. At 7:02, the power flickered. At 7:03, it died.

Customers were already on the sidewalk. A courier in a hurry checked his watch. A retiree peered through the glass. Behind the counter, a barista whispered, "Should we... shut the door?"

The owner exhaled, then stepped outside with a tray of cold brew that hadn't needed electricity and a basket of scones finished before dawn. "We've had a hiccup," she said with a smile. "But I can offer you this now, on the house, and take your order for later. I'll text when we're up." She wrote down names, handed out napkins, and then stopped apologizing—because there was work to do.

Inside, she called the utility, propped the front door open for light, and moved the espresso machine checklist further down the page: *after power returns.*

Same outage. Two possible stories: a ruined opening, or a different kind of opening—one that taught everyone what the café would be like on hard days. The difference was where the owner chose to place her hands.

This is the chapter where we practice that choice.

The Stoic Dichotomy of Control

Epictetus opened his *Handbook* with a truth so clear it still reshapes lives two thousand years later:

"Some things are up to us, and some things are not."

Up to us: our judgments, choices, values, and actions.

Not up to us: the weather, markets, opinions of others, and the outcomes of our efforts.

Most of us live as if the reverse were true. We spend our best hours raging at traffic, resenting bosses, fearing the future, obsessing over likes and comments. The Stoics called this slavery to illusion.

True freedom begins when you draw a line between what is and isn't yours to command. Imagine life as two baskets:

- **In your power**: your judgments, your choices, your actions right now, your tone of voice, your character.

- **Not in your power**: other people's judgments and choices; weather, traffic, markets, algorithms; the past; and final outcomes shaped by many hands.

Confuse the baskets and you suffer twice—first from life's natural difficulty, and second from carrying a weight that was never yours.

This split isn't gloomy; it's liberating. It's the difference between pushing on a locked door and noticing the open gate three steps to the left.

Why This Is So Hard Today

The ancients struggled with gossip, politics, and rumors. We struggle with metrics, notifications, and headlines. The pull on our attention is constant, and most of it lies outside our control.

Modern life sells illusions of control. They feel empowering for a moment but leave us drained.

- **Illusion 1: Algorithms = ownership**

    A post does well, and it feels like mastery. A post sinks, and it feels like erasure. In truth, you influence reach with craft and consistency—you do not control reception.

Stoic move: Aim for quality within your power; measure success by promises kept to your craft.

- **Illusion 2: Metrics = meaning**

  Dashboards are useful—until the numbers start telling you who you are.

  Stoic move: Use metrics to adjust tactics, not to auction off your dignity.

- **Illusion 3: Instant communication = instant control**

  You can message anyone at any time. That doesn't mean you control their attention or mood.

  Stoic move: Ask clearly, set expectations, then let other minds have their own weather.

- **Illusion 4: Personal brand = universal approval**

  Approval is a moving target; chasing it is like building on sand.

  Stoic move: Build character you could live with even in a world without cameras.

- **Illusion 5: News cycle = control cycle**

  Checking headlines feels like action but is often agitation without agency.

Stoic move: Take one action you can own; let the rest be known but not resident.

- **Illusion 6: Anger = power**

    Anger gives a sugar high of certainty, followed by weakness.

    Stoic move: Courage with clarity is strength. Courage without clarity is noise.

Technology blurs the line between what's ours and what's not. Awareness is not control. Information that isn't ours to act on often weighs us down anyway.

Freedom Through Choosing What's Truly Ours

The freedom we're after here isn't political or financial—though those matter. It's inner freedom: the ability to steer your attention, keep your standards, and act with character even when outcomes drift.

The Stoics did not preach passivity. They taught fierce engagement—but only with what is ours to influence.

- **Effort over Outcome**: Aim the arrow, then release attachment to where it lands.

- **Choice over Circumstance**: You can't choose the wind, but you can choose your stance.

- **Values over Validation**: Courage, justice, wisdom, and self-control free you from chasing approval.

For the Stoics, freedom was not the absence of challenge but the clarity of focus. When you live within what is yours, life becomes lighter. The only burdens you carry are the ones you can actually lift.

Practical Exercises for Focus

1. The Two-Column List

Draw two columns: *What's mine / What's not mine.* Fill them honestly for one situation today. Tear off the second column and throw it away.

2. The "Next Clean Step" Rule

When overwhelmed, ask: *What's the next action fully mine to take?* Do that before anything else.

3. The Weather Practice

When facing another person's mood, silently say: *This is weather. I do not control weather.* Then choose your own conduct.

4. The Outcome Fast

For one week, track effort not results. Did I practice? Did I reach out? Did I act fairly? At week's end, notice how peace grows when measured by effort.

5. The "Locked Door" Test

When stuck, ask: *Am I pushing on a locked door?* If yes, stop. Find the open gate.

Reset in Action

Return to the soft opening: By 9:15, the utility truck had arrived. Power returned with a cheer. The first cappuccino hissed into the room like a promise kept. The courier left with a pastry and a grin, the retiree found a window seat, and the chalkboard sign collected fingerprints from happy hands.

The owner added *Thank you for your patience* beneath *soft opening*—not as strategy, but as truth. She had met that morning with the only tools that ever truly belonged to her: attention, tone, and choice.

She hadn't controlled the outage. She had controlled the opening.

Pause and Reflect

- Where this week have I carried the weight of an outcome instead of focusing on my effort?

- What would it look like to place that weight down and return to what's truly mine?

- If my peace depends on things outside my control, will I ever feel secure?

Reset 3 Takeaway

You cannot command the wind, but you can command your aim.

The world will keep offering levers that move nothing: other people's moods, internet applause, the weather of markets and news. Freedom is not found in seizing those. It's found in focusing on what is yours: your judgment, your speech, your next action, your values.

This is your third reset: to reclaim peace by reclaiming focus. To stop chasing what was never yours and to master what always has been—one calm, clean choice at a time.

Yet focus without perspective risks becoming narrow. To stay resilient, you must learn to reframe what you see—to view hardship not as an enemy but as a teacher. That is the work of the next reset: reshaping your lens on the world.

Reset 4

Reframe the World Around You

The power of perspective

The Cracked Window (a parable)

On a Monday morning train, Julia found herself staring at a cracked window. The pane had a spiderweb fracture, fine but unavoidable. She tried to look past it—to the fields sliding by, to the streak of sky—but the fracture split every view.

She muttered: "Of course. This is my commute. A broken window to match a broken week."

Across the aisle, a boy sat with his mother. He leaned toward the glass, tracing the crack with his finger, whispering, "Lightning! Look, Mom, lightning froze here." The mother smiled. The boy laughed every time the light caught the fracture, as if the world had decorated the train just for him.

Same crack. Same train. Two stories unfolding on either side of the aisle. Julia felt her lips twitch toward a smile. She still had her emails, her meeting, her stress. But she realized: the crack wasn't the only thing in the glass. There was also the view.

That morning, nothing outside changed. Only her frame did.

Epictetus on Perspective

The Stoics knew that the world arrives raw, but our mind gives it shape. Epictetus put it bluntly: *"Men are disturbed not by things, but by the views which they take of things."*

Notice what he didn't say. He didn't say nothing is disturbing. He didn't say pain isn't real. He didn't say you can smile away a storm. He said your *view* determines whether you become prisoner or participant.

- Pain exists. Perspective decides if it also becomes despair.
- Delay happens. Perspective decides if it becomes rage.
- Insults fly. Perspective decides if they strike or dissolve.

A frame doesn't erase the picture. It alters the way you see it—and the way you carry it.

Marcus Aurelius reminded himself in his journal: *"Choose not to be harmed—and you won't feel harmed. Don't feel harmed—and you haven't been."* He wasn't denying injury. He was claiming authorship of interpretation.

Seneca compared the mind to a lens: *"We suffer more in imagination than in reality."* Through a warped lens, every inconvenience swells to disaster. Through a trained lens, disaster shrinks back into its actual size.

The Present as Training Ground

Reframing is about the **present moment**—this insult, this delay, this difficulty right now. It is not about rewriting your past (that belongs to Reset 7). It is not about predicting your future (that belongs to Reset 10). It is about here, about this, about training your mind to step back and choose a different angle.

The Stoics practiced this constantly:

- A soldier at the front rephrased "exile" as "a new station."

- A merchant stuck in port reframed "delay" as "time to study."

- A father grieving reminded himself: grief is proof of love, and love is still a good.

The trick is not denial but interpretation. You don't erase reality. You tell a truer, steadier story about it.

Modern Fractures of Perspective

Today's cracks in the window look different, but they split our view just as quickly.

At work:

- A project stalls because someone missed a deadline. You can frame it as proof that "nobody cares," or as a test of your patience and communication.

- A boss criticizes your draft. You can frame it as humiliation, or as free editing.

At home:

- The sink fills again. You can frame it as disrespect, or as a chance to serve without scoreboard.

- A child throws a tantrum. You can frame it as rebellion, or as fatigue, hunger, or confusion.

Online:

- A snide comment arrives. You can frame it as personal attack, or as evidence of the writer's own storm.

- Bad news scrolls across your feed. You can frame it as doom, or as reminder to care for what's near and real.

Every situation has at least two frames. One shrinks you. The other steadies you.

The Three-Step Reframe

The Stoics didn't offer slogans. They offered techniques. Here's a simple reframe drill, repeatable in real life:

1. **Name it cleanly.**

   Strip adjectives, strip blame. "The train is delayed." Not: "This always happens to me."

2. **Add proportion.**

   Zoom out. Will this matter in an hour? A year? A lifetime? Most cracks fade at larger scale.

3. **Choose a lens.**

   Ask: "What interpretation serves my best self here?" Not the most flattering, not the easiest—the one that strengthens you.

Julia on the train practiced this without knowing. Step 1: cracked window. Step 2: just glass, not disaster. Step 3: frame it as lightning art. The commute still happened. But her morning arrived lighter.

Obstacles as Teachers

Marcus Aurelius offered his famous reversal: *"The impediment to action advances action. What stands in the way becomes the way."*

This is the Stoic judo move. Instead of cursing the weight, you use it to grow stronger. Instead of fleeing the friction, you let it train you.

- The angry colleague trains your patience.

- The failed pitch trains your resilience.

- The slow recovery trains your humility.

Life keeps handing you obstacles. Reframing turns them into instructors.

Practices for Perspective

Reframing isn't natural. The first reaction is often panic, anger, or self-pity. But like muscle, the mind trains with repetition.

Daily Reframes to Try:

1. **The Commute Drill.** Each delay, instead of complaint, ask: "What virtue is this training right now—patience, courage, self-control?"

2. **The Inbox Pause.** Before answering a difficult message, write down two possible frames: "attack" vs. "opportunity." Choose the one that strengthens.

3. **The Gratitude Swap.** When you name a problem, force yourself to name a parallel gift. "The sink is full. I have a family to feed."

4. **The Role Flip.** Picture yourself on the other side. How would you see this if you were them? What frame would shrink hostility?

5. **The Ten-Year Test.** Ask: "In ten years, how will I remember this?" A harsh review becomes a blip. A brave act becomes a story.

Each exercise is a rehearsal. Each rehearsal makes the next reframe faster.

Guardrails Against Toxic Positivity

Reframing is not pretending everything is fine. Stoicism is not denial. Some things are genuinely painful. Some cracks hurt.

The difference: Stoics acknowledged pain but refused to add suffering through interpretation. They didn't paint storms pink. They stood in them steady, saying: "This is here. Now, how shall I meet it?"

Healthy reframing asks:

- Is this story true?
- Does it steady me?
- Does it help me act with virtue?

If not, it isn't reframing. It's fantasy.

Reset in Action

Return to Julia on the train. The crack in the window stayed all week. On Friday, a coworker complained about it. Julia said, "Funny—I've been watching lightning dance there all week." The coworker blinked, then laughed. The crack didn't vanish, but its weight did.

That small shift carried into Julia's day. She walked into her meeting calmer, answered critique with more poise, and went home with more energy than she expected. All because she chose one frame over another.

The window was cracked. But her spirit was not.

Reflection Questions

- What crack in my "window" have I been staring at lately?

- What frame am I using—and what other frame could I choose?

- How might this obstacle be training me in patience, courage, or wisdom?

- What will this look like in ten years—or even tomorrow?

Reset 4 Takeaway

Perspective is power. Epictetus taught that it is not events but our judgments that disturb us. Marcus Aurelius insisted that obstacles can become opportunities. Seneca warned that unchecked imagination adds weight to reality.

The world will keep offering cracked windows, delays, and insults. You cannot control the cracks. But you can control your frame.

This is your fourth reset: reframe the world around you. Not to erase hardship, not to deny pain, but to choose the interpretation that steadies you. Present difficulties need not become prisons. With a practiced lens, they can become training grounds.

A steady perspective helps you meet today's obstacles. But perspective alone isn't enough—you also need an anchor. A frame can shift how you see a storm; values decide how you steer through it. That is where the next reset takes us: building a compass sturdy enough to hold when the world wobbles.

Reset 5

Anchor Yourself in Values

The Quiet Compass That Outlasts the Noise

The Promise and the Ping (a parable)

On Monday morning she made herself a promise: no cutting corners this week. The client's deadline was tight, but the work would be honest, the communication clear. She wrote it on a card and slid it under her keyboard.

By Wednesday, the pings began their chorus: a VP's "quick favor," a thread full of blame, a flash sale offering exactly what she wanted when tired. A coworker suggested reusing last quarter's numbers: "No one will notice. We can fix it later." The calendar suggested she was important. The pressure suggested she should bend.

She looked down at the card: *No cutting corners.* She exhaled, wrote, "We'll need to pull current figures; I'll help," and refilled her water. The week didn't get easier. It got clearer.

Noise is loud. Values are quiet. But on the days that make a life, the quiet thing is the stronger thing.

Virtue as the Stoics' Highest Good

The Stoics didn't worship calm; they valued character. Calm follows when character holds.

Their reasoning was sharp:

- Only some things are in our power—our judgments, choices, and actions.
- Virtue—wisdom, justice, courage, self-control—lives in those choices.
- Therefore, virtue is sufficient for a good life.

Not painless, not lucky, not always easy—but good. Because it's built on the only material we fully command: our conduct.

Seneca wrote: *"That which is honourable is the only good"* Marcus Aurelius reminded himself: *"If it is not right, do not do it; if it is not true, do not say it."*

Titles fade. Wealth vanishes. Reputation rises and falls with rumor. But a promise kept is kept. A just act is just. A brave word is brave. Virtue is its own reward.

Anchoring in virtue means you stop outsourcing your compass to the world's incentives, threats, or applause. You hold steady when everything else shakes.

Why Values Matter Today

Modern life is a competition of signals. Metrics, likes, sales, streaks, "urgent" flags—all of them try to tell you what matters. They whisper: *This is important. This is success. This is who you are.*

Without a compass, you drift with these signals. A good day becomes "lots of likes." A bad day becomes "missed a target." You live by dashboards, not direction.

But values cut through noise. They whisper back: *Even if the inbox is full, did you tell the truth? Even if the numbers dip, did you treat people fairly? Even if no one applauds, did you act with courage?*

These questions build a life that lasts longer than metrics.

The Four Virtues, Translated

The Stoics named four cardinal virtues. They can sound lofty, but they come alive when translated into daily acts.

Wisdom → clear seeing

- Fact-check before acting.
- Ask: *What is real? What matters most? What follows from this?*

Justice → fair dealing

- Give credit, pay on time, divide work honestly.
- Ask: *What would be fair if the roles were reversed?*

Courage → brave doing

- Act for the good despite fear. Speak truth early, hold the line, make the hard call.
- Ask: *What would I do here if fear weren't steering?*

Self-control → disciplined choosing

- Guide appetite and impulse so they serve, not rule.
- Ask: *What choice honors my longer aim?*

At work:

- Wisdom is pausing before "reply all."
- Justice is giving credit where it's due.
- Courage is flagging a risk kindly and early.
- Self-control is refusing to over-promise.

At home:

- Wisdom is realizing the fight is really about exhaustion.
- Justice is dividing invisible chores fairly.

- Courage is apologizing first.
- Self-control is closing the laptop when you said you would.

Online:

- Wisdom is checking before you share.
- Justice is refusing to dog-pile.
- Courage is defending someone misrepresented.
- Self-control is stepping away when the thread is a trap for your best hours.

Virtue may sound abstract. In practice, it is ordinary and visible—tiny decisions made steadily.

Building a Personal Compass

A compass is simply a few choices made before you're tired. You consult it when noise rises and willpower thins.

1. **Name Your North (two lines, not a manifesto).**
   - *I aim to be: clear, fair, brave, steady.*
   - *Therefore I will: tell the truth kindly, give credit, keep my word, stop when I've said enough.*

2. Translate Values Into Behaviors.

- Wisdom: Sleep before big decisions; ask one clarifying question per meeting.
- Justice: Document contributions; pay on time.
- Courage: Speak once where silence would be cowardice; make the avoided call.
- Self-control: One phone-free hour daily; one honest stop time each evening.

3. Design Your "No."

Write three sentences in advance:

- "I can't own that outcome, but I can do X by Friday."
- "I'm at capacity; I can help next week."
- "That's outside my role; would you like a referral?"

4. Create a Red Team.

Choose one trusted friend, mentor, or colleague to act as your compass-keeper. Share your two-line compass with them and invite honesty. Once a month, ask: *"Am I still living this?"*

5. Start an Integrity Ledger.

Not for shame—for alignment. Each night, write:

- *Kept: Where did I live my compass?*

- Cost: *What did it cost (time, money, pride)?*
- Worth it? *(Yes/No).*

6. Run Virtue Sprints.

For two weeks, pick one virtue—say Courage. Let it guide decisions. Switch to another. Over a season, all four become familiar muscle groups.

7. Audit the Calendar, Not Just the Conscience.

Look at your last two weeks. If someone saw only your schedule, what would they say you value? Adjust until your time matches your compass.

The Challenge of Noise and Pressure

Modern life is full of pings: metrics, deadlines, side hustles, comment sections. Each whispers: *Bend a little. Nobody will notice.*

This is where values matter most. Anyone can hold a compass when skies are clear. It's when the meeting gets hostile, the inbox grows cruel, or the temptation looks sweet that your anchor proves itself.

What Marcus Aurelius wrote*: "If it is not right, do not do it; if it is not true, do not say it."* It is a sentence small enough to memorize, yet strong enough to hold you when fatigue begs for shortcuts.

Stoic Voices on Character

- Marcus Aurelius urged himself to live by principle, not applause: *"Be content with doing the right thing, and let the world talk."*

- Seneca counseled that wealth, health, and fame are "indifferents." Only virtue makes a person rich.

- Epictetus drilled his students to decide first who they wanted to be, and only then to act. *"First say to yourself what you would be; and then do what you have to do."*

Each Stoic voice harmonizes into one theme: you don't drift into character—you choose it.

Reset in Action

Return to The Promise and the Ping. By Friday, the project was delivered. The client saw only the clean numbers. The coworkers saw teamwork, not the temptation declined. Under the keyboard, the card was worn at the edges but steady in its promise: *No cutting corners.*

The week did not bend her compass. The compass bent the week.

Reflection Questions

- When have I bent under pressure because I wasn't anchored in values?

- What 3–5 values would I want people to see in me even if I lost money, status, or ease?

- How can I make those values visible this week when the pings arrive?

- Who could serve as my "red team," helping me see blind spots?

Reset 5 Takeaway

Noise will always try to bend you. It promises shortcuts, applause, and ease. But it cannot keep its promises.

Values are quieter. They ask you to lose small battles to win the only war that matters: the one for your character.

Marcus Aurelius left a rule you can carry anywhere: *"If it isn't right, don't do it; if it isn't true, don't say it."* Epictetus adds the sequence: *"First decide what you will be; then do what you must do."*

This is your fifth reset: anchor yourself in values. Choose a compass pressure cannot erase, and let that compass define your direction—no matter how loud the noise grows.

A compass sets your direction. But walking that direction demands strength. When pressure grows, it isn't enough to know what matters—you must also have the stamina to endure. The Stoics trained for this not by chasing comfort, but by choosing hardship as practice. That is where we turn next.

Reset 6

Choose Growth Over Comfort

How Voluntary Hardship Strengthens Your Soul

The Broken Elevator (a parable)

On Monday the office elevator broke. By Tuesday, the paper sign—*OUT OF SERVICE*—looked like part of the décor. People traded rumors in the lobby about spare parts and contractors. Most waited, sighed, and stared at their phones like the stairs were a personal insult.

Maya took the stairs. Six floors. The first day, she arrived winded and tried not to show it. The second day, she slung her laptop strap across her chest and left her coffee for after the climb. The third day, she counted flights out loud, quiet enough not to draw looks.

By Friday, the sign was still taped up. So were the stairs. They no longer felt hostile. Maya reached the landing, not fresh but steady, and noticed two things: her breath arrived sooner, and her mood arrived kinder.

No one had fixed the elevator. But the stairs had fixed something in her—something not broken, just underused.

That week taught her a lesson with a long echo: friction can be a teacher. Sometimes the world removes comforts; sometimes you remove them yourself. Either way, you become different by meeting the climb.

This chapter is about choosing some climbs on purpose.

Seneca on Voluntary Hardship

Seneca lived among gardens, villas, and tutors. Wealth surrounded him, but he refused to let luxury make him fragile. Comfort, he warned, is never guaranteed. If your peace depends on cushions, it vanishes the moment fortune rearranges the furniture.

So Seneca advised his students to practice discomfort in small doses. His drills were plain:

- Live simply on purpose. For a few days, wear rough clothes and eat the scantiest fare. Then ask: *Is this what I feared?*

- Let the body feel weather. Endure heat, cold, or exertion without complaint—not to harm yourself, but to remind yourself you are sturdier than you imagine.

- Rehearse adversity in the mind. Picture losses and disruptions before they come. Not to brood, but so misfortune feels familiar if it ever knocks.

Seneca's point was sharp:

- If you only function in comfort, you will collapse in discomfort.

- If you train in discomfort, you will stand when others fall.

He put it bluntly: *"Calamity is virtue's opportunity."* Hardship is the stage where character performs.

Why Growth and Comfort Rarely Coexist

Comfort is not evil. Warmth, ease, and safety have their place. But the Stoics warned: constant comfort shrinks our capacity.

Think of muscles: unused, they weaken. Stressed under weight, they grow. The same holds true for resilience, patience, discipline, and courage.

There are two kinds of ease:

- **Earned ease** — the peace that follows training, clarity, and wise systems.

- **Unexamined ease** — the comfort that numbs, narrows, and quietly taxes your future.

Stoicism sides with the first and distrusts the second.

The Tax of Constant Comfort

Comfort creep is subtle. We smooth away every bump until the smallest delay feels like disaster. A slow page load sparks outrage. A cool room feels like an insult. A skipped snack feels like an emergency.

When the world must always match your preferences, your freedom shrinks to the size of your settings. And when life removes even one cushion, the fall feels fatal.

The Gift of Chosen Discomfort

Growth hides in friction. The moments that stretch us—delays, failures, hard conversations—are not punishments but training partners.

When you practice saying *no* to a craving, *yes* to a hill, or *later* to a screen, you widen your window for everything else. Everyday annoyances stop renting space in your head so cheaply. You carry yourself differently—less fragile, more steady, more available to those who need you.

A Warning Against Performance

Voluntary hardship is not about bragging rights. If discomfort becomes a contest, it stops training character and starts feeding vanity. The goal is capacity: steady, useful, repeatable.

Before any drill, ask:

1. Does this serve the person I am trying to become?

2. Is the dose challenging but not reckless?

If either answer is no, adjust. The point is growth, not spectacle.

Practices for Resilience

The Stoics practiced hardship in simple, deliberate ways. We can do the same today.

1. Fasting

- *Ancient*: Seneca skipped meals to test his fear of poverty.

- *Modern*: Try intermittent fasting, or skip one meal a week.

- *Lesson*: Hunger rises, then falls. You remain. Appetite need not be your master.

2. Digital Restraint

- *Ancient*: The Stoics avoided gossip and idle chatter.

- *Modern*: Take a two-hour phone-free block daily, or one social-media-free day a week.

- *Lesson*: Your peace is not owned by algorithms. Attention is yours.

3. Cold Showers or Physical Endurance

- *Ancient*: Cold baths, heat, long marches.

- *Modern*: Take a cold shower, walk instead of driving, or exercise without headphones.

- *Lesson*: Discomfort rarely lasts as long as the mind predicts.

4. Saying No to Minor Luxuries

- *Ancient*: Eating coarse bread when feasts were available.

- *Modern*: Delay that impulse purchase; skip soda for water; leave the favorite snack untouched for a week.

- *Lesson*: Desire shrinks when you prove you don't always obey it.

5. Voluntary Simplicity

- *Ancient*: Plain clothes, simple meals, walking instead of being carried.

- *Modern*: Spend a weekend without conveniences—cook from scratch, dress simply, sit without background noise.

- *Lesson*: Life feels lighter when you prove you need less.

6. The "Harder Path" Habit

Once a day, choose the slightly harder route: take stairs, walk instead of calling, speak the truth instead of deflecting. Each choice trains resilience.

7. Controlled Exposure to Fear

Write down a fear—public speaking, asking for help, saying no. Take one small step into it. Each repetition turns dread into familiarity.

Stoic Voices on Hardship

- **Epictetus** reminded his students: *"Difficulties show what men are."* Hardship is not an interruption but a revelation.

- **Seneca** told Lucilius: *"Set aside a certain number of days, during which you shall be content with the scantiest and cheapest fare, with coarse and rough dress, saying to yourself: Is this the condition I feared?"*

- **Marcus Aurelius** wrote in *Meditations*: *"The impediment to action advances action. What stands in the way becomes the way."* He was not celebrating obstacles for their own sake but showing how adversity can redirect us into strength.

Reset in Action

Return to the broken elevator. By the next Monday, it was repaired. Maya could have gone back to convenience. But she chose the stairs twice a week. It was no longer about machinery. It was about training her resilience.

Each climb reminded her: growth often begins where comfort ends. The elevator may have been fixed, but her strength had been built on the stairs.

Reflection Questions

- Where in my life have I avoided discomfort out of habit, not necessity?

- What small voluntary hardship could I choose this week to remind myself I'm stronger than I think?

- How might my confidence grow if I trained with discomfort instead of fleeing it?

- Which comforts feel harmless but are quietly shrinking my capacity?

Choose Growth Over Comfort

Reset 6 Takeaway

You cannot build resilience in constant ease. Some discomfort must be chosen.

Seneca's counsel was not that pain is noble, but that you are sturdier than the cushions the world sells you. Voluntary hardship is a way of telling your nervous system the truth:

- You can wait a little.

- You can carry a little.

- You can hear *no* without breaking.

- You can say *no* without cruelty.

- You can be uncomfortable and still be yourself.

Marcus Aurelius, Seneca, and Epictetus each trained this posture daily. They knew storms would come. They refused to arrive untrained.

Let small, chosen fires temper you. Then, when unchosen heat arrives, you will not burn—you will bear. You will even brighten, for yourself and for those who walk beside you.

This is your sixth reset: choose growth over comfort. Meet the stairs of life with steady breath. Let voluntary hardship enlarge your capacity. So when fortune removes a cushion, you will already know how to stand.

Reset 7

Release What Weighs You Down

How Forgiveness Frees Your Spirit

The Stone in the Pack (a parable)

Two hikers set out before dawn. The air was sharp, the trail winding, the ridge promising a view worth the climb. Their packs carried the essentials—water, food, maps. Yet one hiker added something extra: a smooth stone, heavy enough to notice but small enough to excuse.

"Why?" his friend asked.

"It reminds me of what he said," the hiker replied, thinking of an insult from weeks ago. "I'll carry it to remember."

As the morning warmed, the pack grew heavier. Soon he added another stone—something a colleague had done years before, never apologized for. By noon, his shoulders ached, and his pace slowed. His friend, lighter and freer, said: "Let's rest at the stream."

At the water's edge, the hiker opened his pack. The stones stared back at him—silent reminders of grudges disguised as companions.

"If I drop them," he said, "it means what happened was okay."

His friend shook his head gently. "No. It means you'll reach the ridge. The stones don't make the past true. They only make the present harder."

The hiker stood a long while, listening to the water. One by one, he lifted the stones and let them fall. The mountain was no shorter. But his back—freed from the weight he had chosen to keep—was stronger for the climb.

Chains of Yesterday: Grudges, Envy, Comparison, Anger

The Stoics warned about a trap that looks like strength: clutching hurts, replaying injuries, or measuring your life against someone else's. Each of these postures seems like armor. In truth, they are chains.

Grudges — a rope you keep pulling.
They rehearse the past as if that could change it. Marcus Aurelius offered the clean release: *"The best revenge is not to be like your enemy."* A grudge is the worst kind of inheritance—you keep reliving someone else's act long after they've forgotten it.

Envy — a crooked teacher.
It whispers: *"They have what should be mine."* But envy shrinks your world to another person's plot of land. Stoicism suggests: let envy instruct your work. Translate jealousy into

admiration and practice, so it becomes growth fuel rather than corrosion.

Comparison — the wrong ruler.
It tempts us to measure progress by others' timing: their career, their possessions, their body, their applause. But the Stoic counter is clear: measure against your own growth. *Am I truer today than last week? Kinder this afternoon than yesterday morning?*

Anger — the fire that burns the holder.
Seneca warned: *"Anger, if not restrained, is more hurtful to us than the injury that provokes it."* Anger promises strength but usually hands your peace to the very person you resent. It punishes you first, long before it touches anyone else.

These weights all masquerade as tools: a grudge to remind you, envy to motivate you, comparison to measure you, anger to defend you. But in practice, they only add stones to your pack.

Forgiveness as Strength

Forgiveness in Stoicism is not amnesia or permission. It is clarity—the act of dropping stones that never helped you climb.

What Forgiveness Is Not

- **Not forgetting.** Memory remains, but the sting need not.

- **Not reconciliation.** That requires two people; forgiveness requires only your stance.

- **Not boundaryless.** You can forgive and still lock the door.

What Forgiveness Is

- **A refusal to become what you despise.** Marcus Aurelius reminded himself: *"The wrongdoer has done you no harm, because he has not made you more unjust."*

- **A clean break with rumination.** Choosing not to rehearse the same injury each morning.

- **A return of power.** By releasing the past, you reclaim your energy for the present.

Epictetus reminded his students: people act from mistaken opinions. Teach them if you can, bear them if you must—but don't poison yourself in the process.

Boundaries With Compassion

Forgiveness does not mean naivety. You can say *no* without hatred and *yes* without fear. You can keep your heart unarmed while your door remains locked.

Stoicism invites us to practice this paradox: a stance that is both guarded and gentle, both firm and free of venom.

Pocket lines:

- *I will not pay interest on a pain I did not choose.*
- *The wrong is theirs; my stance is mine.*
- *Release is strength, not weakness.*

Practical Exercises for Release and Renewal

These are not theories but small practices you can try when stones feel heavy.

1. **The Grudge Audit (10 min, once)**

    Divide a page into: *Grievance / Cost*. List the injury, then what it costs (sleep, focus, trust). Finish with: *I choose not to spend ____ on ____ anymore.*

2. **The Stone Ritual (3 min, as needed)**

    Hold a stone in your hand and name the resentment aloud. Then drop it into water or soil. As the stone leaves your hand, let your body mirror your mind: you have chosen release.

3. **Letter You Won't Send (15 min)**

    Write the full story as if you were telling it to the person. Then decide: burn it to release it, save it for your own clarity, or reduce it to three calm sentences if a real conversation is needed.

4. Envy to Admiration (5 min)

When envy stirs, pause and ask: *What is it that I truly admire here?* Then translate that insight into one small action you can adopt in your own life. In this way, envy becomes a teacher, not a thief.

5. The Comparison Fast (one week)

Choose one area—career, possessions, or body—and step away from social feeds in that domain for a full week. Each night, write down one thing you did that aligned with your own values. By the end, you'll notice how much lighter life feels when measured by your compass, not by others' timelines.

6. Nightly Release (one line)

Before bed, write one line: *What did I carry today that wasn't mine?* Close the notebook and let sleep finish the release.

Stoic Voices on Letting Go

- Marcus Aurelius: *"Reject the sense of injury, and the injury itself disappears."*

- Seneca: *"It is better to heal than to seek revenge—for revenge keeps wounds open, but forgiveness allows them to close."*

- Epictetus: *"Remember, it is not he who reviles you or strikes you who insults you, but your opinion that these things are insulting."*

Each line pulls the same direction: freedom lies not in erasing the past, but in refusing to let it script your present.

Reset in Action

Return to the hikers: the stones did not erase the past. The events still happened. But the hiker no longer bore them. His pack carried only what was useful—food, water, tools for the climb.

Our stones are invisible but no less real: the argument replayed at night, the bitterness over someone else's success, the old self-criticism we nurse. The reset is simple: open the pack. Name one stone. Ask: *Does this move me forward, or weigh me down?* If it weighs you down, set it in the stream.

Reflection Questions

- What stone am I carrying today—and what is it costing me?

- Where am I measuring myself by others instead of my own growth?

- What would forgiveness look like here, without excusing harm?

- How could I turn envy into admiration + action this week?

Reset 7 Takeaway

Grudges, envy, comparison, and anger promise power but deliver chains. Forgiveness promises loss but delivers freedom—freedom of attention, dignity, and choice.

You cannot climb far if your pack is full of stones. The past cannot be changed, but it can be remembered rightly: what belongs to you (your conduct), what belongs to others (their choices), and what belongs to time (everything already finished).

This is your seventh reset: release what weighs you down. Forgiveness is not weakness; it is strength. Comparison is not fuel; it is theft. Set the stones down, and carry only what you need for the climb ahead.

Letting go of the past creates space, but space without rhythm quickly fills again. If yesterday's burdens are released, today's hours must be guided. The Stoics knew that steadiness isn't just about dropping weight—it's about creating rhythms that protect your calm each day. That is where the next reset turns.

Reset 8

Build Daily Rituals for Calm

How Small Rhythms Protect Your Peace

The Three Bells (a parable)

On the first workday of the year, a city maintenance worker climbed into the old clock tower. He polished brass, tightened bolts, checked wiring. The last addition wasn't for timekeeping: three small bronze bells, set to ring softly at dawn, noon, and dusk.

They weren't meant to compete with the thunder of the main bells. They were reminders—gentle nudges in the middle of noise. Most of the city never noticed them. Traffic drowned them; conversations kept moving. But one woman heard them.

At the first bell, she put her phone down and stood by the window, taking slow, fuller breaths. At the second, she stopped juggling tabs and returned to the one task she had promised to finish. At the third, she wrote a single line about what she was carrying that wasn't hers—and set it down for the night.

Deadlines stayed crowded. The world stayed noisy. But the three bells stitched her days with calm, marking seams between rush and rest.

This chapter is about hanging your own bells—daily rituals that shape how you meet the hours.

Why Rhythm Matters

The Stoics valued rhythm more than ritual. Not pomp or ceremony, but quiet habits that tuned the mind as predictably as a musician tunes an instrument. Marcus Aurelius primed his mind at dawn; Epictetus urged students to stop mid-day and examine themselves; Seneca closed each evening with a private audit.

They understood what psychology confirms today: the brain leans on rhythm. Without deliberate patterns, attention drifts to the loudest voice in the room. With them, calm becomes muscle memory.

Calm found once (Reset 1) is a victory. Calm kept through rhythm is a life.

Morning: Begin With Intention

The morning sets the tone for every hour that follows. Most of us let the day write its script before we have chosen a word. The Stoics practiced the opposite: they wrote the first lines deliberately.

Three elements of a Stoic morning:

- **A line of intention.** One sentence on paper: *"Today I aim to be patient."* Or *"I won't trade peace for speed."* Small, but directional.

- **Breath before screens.** Ten slow breaths before touching your phone or email. The pause tells your body: presence first, not reaction.

- **Expectation of friction.** Marcus Aurelius reminded himself each morning: today he would meet arrogance, selfishness, envy. This wasn't pessimism; it was inoculation. By expecting challenge, he reduced its power to surprise him.

A calm morning is not a promise of an easy day. It is armor woven in silence before the battles begin.

Mid-Day: Return to Yourself

Strong mornings still fray. Drift happens quietly—by noon, most of us are scattered across messages, tasks, moods. That's why Stoics practiced *recollection.*

Three elements of a Stoic mid-day reset:

- **Pause-and-breathe minute.** Three deep breaths. Ask: *"Am I choosing, or just reacting?"*

- **Re-anchor in a virtue.** Write one word on a slip of paper—Wisdom, Justice, Courage, Self-control. Let that word steer your next decision.

- **Simplify the field.** Pick one task to finish. Stoics knew scattered energy dilutes strength. One clean completion steadies more than five half-finished sprints.

A mid-day ritual is like tightening the knot of a tent rope. It keeps the whole structure steady when winds pick up.

Evening: Review and Release

Seneca described closing each day with a private conversation with his conscience. Not scolding, but training. He asked what he had done well, where he had failed, and what he would adjust tomorrow.

Three elements of a Stoic evening:

- **One-line release.** For instance, write: *"Today I carried worry about tomorrow's meeting. Now, I set it down for the night."* Naming the burden and closing it with intention signals to your mind that rest is allowed.

- **One lesson forward.** Instead of brooding over mistakes, capture a single takeaway: *"Next time, pause before replying."*

- **Gratitude as grounding.** List three specifics—no matter how small: a meal you enjoyed, a shared laugh, a breath of fresh air. Gratitude lightens the weight of the day without pretending it was easy.

Evening rituals stitch closure into restless hours. Without them, days blur. With them, you carry forward wisdom instead of fatigue.

Journaling as a Stoic Tool

The Stoics were among history's first journalers. Marcus Aurelius never intended his *Meditations* for publication; they were reminders to himself. Seneca's letters doubled as personal audits. Epictetus had his students keep notes of daily practices.

What Stoic journaling is not:

- Not a diary of events.

- Not a record for others.

- Not an exercise in eloquence.

What it is:

- A discipline of thought.

- A way to slow impressions until they can be tested.

- A private space where clarity is rehearsed.

Three formats to try:

- **The one-line journal.** Morning: *What matters most today?* Mid-day: *Where am I losing focus?* Night: *What did I do well, and what will I adjust?*

- **The question journal.** Ask daily: *What is mine? What is not?* The answers cut through clutter.

- **The practice journal.** Track one act of Wisdom, Justice, Courage, and Self-control each day. Over time, the pattern shows strengths to keep, gaps to close.

Writing slows thought just enough for choice. Without capture, impressions swirl endlessly. With capture, they can be tested, reframed, or released.

Living Wisdom as Rhythm, Not Theory

Epictetus said: *"Don't explain your philosophy. Embody it."* Rituals are embodiment—ideas made flesh through repetition.

What rhythm looks like:

- Virtues set the beat: Wisdom, Justice, Courage, Self-control.

- Small and repeatable: better to pause twenty times today than retreat once a year.

- Stitched days, not scattered hours: intention at dawn, correction at noon, release at dusk.

Why rhythm works:

- It trims clutter before it calcifies into resentment.
- It builds a steady floor under unpredictable events.
- It gives calm a body—not a mood you chase, but a rhythm you practice.

Practical Exercises for Daily Calm

1. **The 3×3 Rule.** Three breaths at dawn, three at noon, three at night. Anchors without overwhelm.

2. **Bell Reminders.** Set gentle alarms (not harsh buzzers) at key times. When they ring, pause.

3. **One-Word Anchors.** Choose a daily word: *Steady, Clear, Kind.* Whisper it when you drift.

4. **End-of-Day Audit.** Write two lines: *Kept: where I lived my compass. Missed: where I drifted.* Tomorrow, aim to shorten the "missed."

5. **Weekly Ritual Reset.** Each Sunday, review your rituals. Which stitched calm? Which frayed? Adjust one at a time.

Reset in Action

Return to the three bells. The inbox filled, traffic snarled, deadlines pressed. But each soft chime pulled her back: breathe, focus, release. We may not have bells in a tower, but we can hang our own—calendar nudges, sticky notes, one-line journals.

Their power isn't in volume. It's in rhythm. Three times a day, they brought her back to herself until calm was no longer something she chased but something she practiced.

Reflection Questions

- What small ritual could I add tomorrow morning that would anchor my stance?

- Where mid-day do I tend to lose myself—and what could be my "bell" to return?

- What is one evening practice that would help me release instead of rehearse?

- How would my days feel if I stitched them with rhythm, not reaction?

Reset 8 Takeaway

Calm is not a mood you wait for; it's a rhythm you build. Morning intention, mid-day reset, evening reflection—together they stitch wisdom into your hours.

Seneca reminds us: each day brings gifts; rituals are how you unwrap them. Marcus Aurelius reminds us: disturbances come from judgments; daily practices let you revise them in real time. Epictetus would nod at the simplicity: start with what is yours; act; release; repeat.

This is your eighth reset: hang your own bells. Let them ring softly three times a day. When they do, breathe, write one line, choose the next clean step. Calm is not waiting for you somewhere else. It is waiting for you in rhythm.

Rituals stabilize the self. But a steady self still lives among others. The Stoics never imagined philosophy as isolation; they saw it as service. After you have stitched calm into your own hours, the next step is to extend that steadiness outward—into community, relationships, and the hive you belong to.

Reset 9

Strength Through Connection

Why Service and Community Strengthen Your Soul

The Bridge on Maple Street (a parable)

The little bridge on Maple Street wasn't much—just a span over the creek where kids launched leaf boats in spring. After a storm, a fallen limb wedged under the railing and clogged the flow. Water spilled into the park, swallowing the path. People stood at the tape, sighed, and detoured the long way around.

Saturday morning, an older man in a blue cap arrived with a rake and a thermos. He waded to his shins and tugged branches loose. A teenage runner slowed, then hopped down to help. A dog walker tied his leash to the fence and climbed in, boots and all. Strangers minutes before, they formed a chain, passing waterlogged sticks to the grass.

By noon, the creek ran free. The park drained. The city would send a crew Monday, but Maple Street was open now because three people chose to be citizens instead of spectators. The traffic still hummed. The news still scrolled. The world didn't transform. But a pocket of it did. And each person went home lighter, less alone, more themselves.

This reset is about that posture: Stoicism as service. Not withdrawal. Not self-absorption. But steadiness turned outward—living like part of the hive.

Stoicism Is Not Isolation — It's Service

Stoicism is often miscast as detachment: a sage on a mountain, untouched by the mess of ordinary life. But the real Stoics lived in courts, homes, marketplaces, and armies. They wrote not to flee the world but to endure and improve it.

Marcus Aurelius ruled an empire in constant flux, yet reminded himself daily to meet people without bitterness. Epictetus, born enslaved, taught that freedom of spirit was the first step to treating others justly. Seneca wrote letters urging philosophy not as decoration but as duty: how to live rightly among others.

The Stoic stance is not "I don't need anyone." It is: "Because I don't cling, I am free to serve." Service is not a burden. It is the highest expression of freedom—your best self, put to use.

Marcus Aurelius: The Hive and the Bee

Marcus Aurelius wrote: *"What is not good for the hive is not good for the bee."*

This isn't just metaphor—it's biology. A bee apart from the hive doesn't become freer; it becomes lost. Likewise, a person who rejects community starves essential parts of themselves: belonging, accountability, meaning.

The hive image also guards against two distortions of modern life:

- **Harsh individualism**, which glorifies independence and mistakes help for weakness.

- **Foggy collectivism**, which hides behind the crowd and dodges personal duty.

The Stoic middle holds both truths: you are accountable for your conduct, and you are part of something larger that shapes—and is shaped by—that conduct.

A practical test for action: *If everyone copied this tomorrow, would our shared life improve or decay?* Adjust accordingly.

Relationships, Community, and Empathy Today

Expecting difficulty

Marcus Aurelius began *Meditations* by warning himself: "Today you will meet the meddling, the arrogant, the envious, the unsocial." He wasn't cynical—he was preparing. Expecting difficulty helps us meet people without surprise or poison.

Empathy as discipline

For Stoics, empathy is not sentimental indulgence; it is accurate care. It means: *I see you as human, I share your frailty, and I will choose conduct that preserves both our dignity.*

Three disciplines of empathy

1. **Role clarity**: With a colleague, act as a colleague. With a child, act as a parent. With a friend, act as a friend. Each role carries its own duties.

2. **Shared frailty**: Assume the unseen—fear, fatigue, history. Aim your tone accordingly.

3. **Boundaries + kindness**: You can be compassionate and boundaried in the same sentence.

Modern empathy without burnout

- When someone vents: listen once, reflect back one fact or feeling, then steady yourself. Don't absorb every spark.

- When you help: state clearly what you can offer—time, skill, presence—without promising what isn't yours.

- When you can't help: say so plainly. Clarity is kinder than vanishing.

Community in Practice

Stoic philosophy shows up in small rooms, not just in history books.

- **At work**: steadiness under stress steadies the team. A calm person anchors the room.

- **At home**: patience plus boundaries makes love durable. A fair word today prevents bitterness tomorrow.

- **Online**: sometimes justice means speaking up; sometimes it means stepping away.

The common thread: community is built not by speeches but by consistent conduct.

Journaling and Reflection: The Inner Connection That Serves Others

Self-reflection in Stoicism was not self-indulgence; it was self-maintenance. Marcus Aurelius wrote to himself so he wouldn't spread bitterness. Seneca's letters doubled as self-audits.

Try three short lines a day:

- Morning: "Today I will bring patience into this room."
- Mid-day: "What isn't mine to carry?"
- Evening: "Where did I treat someone as kin—and where did I forget?"

Clarity with yourself protects others from your unexamined moods.

Living Wisdom as Rhythm, Not Theory

Epictetus warned: *"Don't explain your philosophy. Embody it."* Service is not a single act but a rhythm stitched into days:

- A pause before snapping.
- A breath before answering.
- A question before acting: *What serves the hive here?*

Wisdom leaves the page and enters the room through rhythm, not theory.

Practical Exercises for Connection

1. The Hive Check

Each evening, ask: *What did I do today that served the hive? Where did I forget?* Write one line for each.

2. The Empathy Pause

When irritated, silently say: *They act from what they know. I too act poorly at times.* Then choose conduct with dignity.

3. The Contribution Shift

Instead of asking, *What did I get today?* ask, *What did I give?*—patience, clarity, fairness, presence.

4. The Circle of Impact

List three people in your life. For each, write: *What would serving them look like today?* Small, doable actions only.

5. The Shared Burden Practice

When you feel overwhelmed, ask: *Who else can carry part of this?* Service flows both ways—accepting help strengthens community.

Modern Parallels

Connection in the twenty-first century looks different but carries the same Stoic weight.

- **Neighborhoods**: clearing a storm drain, helping with groceries, or simply greeting others builds micro-hives.

- **Digital spaces**: posting responsibly, resisting outrage bait, and amplifying truth are forms of service.

- **Global crises**: while one person cannot fix climate change or injustice, one can reduce harm, support efforts, and influence circles of trust.

The Stoic approach reframes these not as optional kindnesses but as duties of shared humanity.

Reset in Action

Return to Maple Street: the creek didn't unclog itself. The city crew hadn't come. The bridge was cleared because strangers chose to act like bees in the hive. None saved the city. But each saved a pocket of it—and in doing so, strengthened themselves.

So too with us. You will not fix the whole world. But you can clear one branch, ease one burden, brighten one room. Service doesn't diminish you; it deepens you.

Reflection Questions

- Where in my life am I acting like the bee apart from the hive?

- Who around me could use steadiness more than speeches this week?

- If my conduct were copied tomorrow, would the hive be healthier or weaker?

- How can I practice empathy without burning out?

Reset 9 Takeaway

Strength is not isolation; it is connection. Marcus Aurelius reminds us: *"What is not good for the hive is not good for the bee."*

Stoic practice—steady breath, clear judgment, the next clean act—was never meant to stop with you. It equips you to be good company in other people's lives: a steady person shifts the weather of a room; a fair person steadies a team; a brave person lifts someone weaker.

The hive and the bee are not at odds. What is good for the hive—truth, fairness, courage, self-control—nourishes you too. Service is not self-erasure. It is character in motion.

The Calm Within

This is your ninth reset: act like part of the hive. Trade bitterness for presence, selfishness for service, and isolation for the strength of connection.

Living as part of the hive gives strength for today. But tomorrow will always arrive with its fog, its uncertainty, its shifting ground. The final test of calm is not found in community alone, but in how you face what lies ahead when the horizon is unclear. For that, you need courage—disciplined, steady, and prepared.

Reset 10

Face the Future with Courage

Finding Balance Amid Uncertainty and Change

The Lantern in the Fog (a parable)

The ferry left the harbor before dawn. Out past the breakwater, fog folded the world to the length of the deck. Passengers clustered by the rail as if distance could be forced from mist. A boy asked the captain if the boat had high beams, like the kind that cut tunnels in the dark on the freeway.

The captain smiled. "Headlights don't help on the water," she said. "We use a lantern."

"A lantern?" the boy laughed. "For all this?"

She held one up: small, steady, unimpressed by the fog. "I don't need to see the whole ocean. I need to see the next ten feet, and the instruments that help me keep my bearing."

She checked the compass, the depth finder, the clock. She knew the tide chart by heart. She moved slow, and cleanly, and didn't argue with the weather. An hour later, the fog thinned and the island rose like a promise kept—not because the world got certain, but because the captain kept her discipline when it wasn't.

This reset is about that lantern—about steering a life when the future refuses to be a freeway.

Uncertainty and Change as Constants

The Stoics began with a sobering but liberating truth: life is uncertain. Empires rise and fall, health breaks, friendships end, fortunes turn. Nothing is guaranteed except change.

Seneca counseled: *"Every new beginning comes from some other beginning's end"*

Marcus Aurelius reminded himself daily: *"Observe constantly that all things take place by change, and that Nature loves nothing so much as to make new things like them."*

Epictetus gave the compass line: *"Some things are in our control, others not."*

The point was not despair but preparation. If uncertainty is guaranteed, then clinging to certainty is suffering. Instead, the Stoics trained for adaptability—building an inner posture that does not collapse when the world shifts.

We often talk about "when things settle down," as if the ocean owes us a glassy surface. It doesn't. Markets swell and dip. Technologies arrive like weather fronts. People enter and leave our lives. Bodies change. Plans collide with other plans. The Stoics did not treat this as a glitch in the system. They treated it as the system itself.

The Mind's Bad Deals with the Future

Modern life tempts us into three bad bargains that deepen our unease:

1. Prediction addiction

We convince ourselves that if we analyze hard enough, certainty will appear. It won't. Forecasts can guide, but they never guarantee.

2. Catastrophe theater

We rehearse disasters in our heads until panic feels like preparation. In reality, we're just suffering twice.

3. Control creep

We try to micromanage what belongs to others—their choices, moods, and timing. Resentment grows, influence shrinks.

Each of these habits weakens us. They trade peace for illusions.

The Stoic Counter-Offer

The Stoics propose a cleaner exchange:

- **Trade prediction for preparation.** You cannot foresee every storm, but you can carry a compass.

- **Trade panic rehearsal for practice.** Train small acts of courage, patience, and self-control daily.

- **Trade control for conduct.** You can't script the world, but you can choose your stance within it.

Three truths summarize the Stoic posture:

1. The future is a range, not a line. Work with scenarios, not fantasies of single outcomes.

2. Change will visit, invited or not. Treat it as design, not defect.

3. Character travels. Roles, jobs, and tools may change, but courage, justice, wisdom, and self-control fit everywhere.

Everyday Scenes of Uncertainty

Uncertainty isn't abstract; it lives in your inbox, your body, and your bank account:

- **At work**: a new software rollout disrupts your routine. You can't freeze the update. You can learn the essentials and keep your skills portable.

- **In relationships**: a friend grows distant. You cannot script their heart. You can keep warmth in yours, ask once with sincerity, and build a life with other sources of connection.

- **In money matters**: savings wobble with the market. You cannot bully the graphs. You can maintain your contribution, your discipline, and your calm.

These aren't glitches to erase. They are invitations to grow steadier.

To live is to navigate fog. The calm Stoicism teaches is not a bet on stable conditions—it's a discipline for unstable ones. The world will always shift. Your job is not to demand clarity from the horizon, but to carry a lantern bright enough for the next ten feet.

Memento Mori: Preparing for Adversity and Mortality

Few ideas strike modern ears as harder than the Stoic practice of *memento mori*: remember that you must die. But for the Stoics, this was not morbid—it was clarifying.

Marcus Aurelius wrote: *"You could leave life right now. Let that determine what you do and say and think."*

Seneca told his friend Lucilius: *"It is not that we have a short time to live, but that we waste much of it."*

Epictetus counseled: *"Let death and exile, and all other things which appear terrible, be daily before your eyes... so you will never entertain any abject thought."*

The most honest Stoic sentence is short: *we are mortal.*

The most loving Stoic sentence is its partner: *remembering this helps you live.*

Memento mori is not brooding—it is a corrective lens. It sharpens kindness, trims cowardice, and makes priorities walk upright.

What *memento mori* changes:

- Time becomes precious, not scarce. Scarcity panics; preciousness prioritizes.

- Petty wars lose soldiers. Grudges and performative busyness can't justify their payroll under this light.

- Courage rises. You tell the truth earlier, love more openly, and stop outsourcing your life to "later."

Premeditatio Malorum: Rehearsing Adversity Without Poisoning the Day

The Stoics also practiced *premeditatio malorum*—the premeditation of hardships. Not to summon sorrow, but to rehearse courage. You picture plausible difficulties and plan your stance in advance.

A simple pattern:

1. Name one hard thing that might visit. (A project fails. A flight cancels. A diagnosis comes.)

2. Name the virtue it will ask for. (Courage, patience, justice, self-control.)

3. Name the first clean act you would take. (Call, clarify, breathe, gather facts, ask for help.)

Then set the thought down and return to your day. You haven't called the storm; you've packed a raincoat.

Far from darkening life, this lens brightens it. The awareness of limits makes every ordinary day luminous. Death sets the clock; adversity sets the weather. What remains is your stance—and your stance is always yours to choose.

Building Courage for What Lies Ahead

Courage is not the absence of fear. It is the decision—trained and repeatable—to act with fear when something good requires it.

The Stoics tucked courage among their four virtues because it enables the others: wisdom sees, justice aims, self-control steadies, and courage moves.

For them, courage meant three things:

1. **Facing reality clearly**—not denying pain, risk, or mortality, but refusing to exaggerate them.

2. **Acting in alignment with virtue**—choosing what is right even when it is costly.

3. **Practicing steadiness daily**—training in small acts of courage so larger ones don't overwhelm you.

Modern courage looks much the same:

- Asking for fair pay with data and a steady voice, even if your heart thumps.

- Saying "I'm sorry" first, cleanly, without a jury speech.

- Declining the lucrative lie and offering the honest version instead.

- Accepting a diagnosis without surrendering your dignity.

- Raising children in an uncertain world with steadiness, not fear.

How courage grows:

- **Exposure, then recovery**: Do the small hard thing, rest, repeat. Like weight training for the will.

- **Clarity before charge**: Name what you're doing for—truth, fairness, love. Courage needs a reason.

- **Company helps**: Bravery is contagious when you keep brave people near.

Practical Exercises for Courage

1. The Five Conversations List

Write down five talks you've been avoiding—an ask, a boundary, an apology, feedback, goodbye. Start with the easiest this week.

2. The Ten-Second Window

When a brave act is called for, exhale, name the virtue you want to serve, and act before hesitation takes the wheel.

3. The Risk-on-Purpose Habit

Once a month, take one constructive risk—pitch, publish, invite, apply. Courage is easier when it has an appointment.

4. The Lantern Drill

Each morning, write one "lantern step"—the next clean action that moves you forward. No headlights, no entire ocean—just the next ten feet.

5. The Mortality Reminder

Each evening, ask: *If today had been my last, what would I be glad I did? What would I regret?* Adjust tomorrow accordingly.

Reset in Action

Return to the ferry: The fog didn't clear because the passengers willed it to. The island didn't arrive faster because anyone worried. What carried them was the captain's posture: one lantern, one compass, one steady pace.

In your own life, you don't need high beams that erase uncertainty. You need a lantern—simple daily practices, a compass of values, and the discipline to keep moving even when the horizon is hidden.

Fog will come again, but you'll be ready.

Reflection Questions

- Where do I demand certainty before I act?
- What is one area where I can practice moving forward with "a lantern, not headlights"?
- How does remembering mortality change the way I treat my time today?
- What small act of courage could I practice this week?

Reset 10 Takeaway

You cannot erase uncertainty, but you can meet it with courage. The Stoics remind us: life is foggy, fragile, finite. The future will not hand you guarantees.

Courage, then, is not about stilling the sea but about holding the wheel. It is remembering you are temporary—not to chill your blood, but to warm your choices. It is considering adversity before it knocks, so you can meet it clothed and upright. It is practicing small acts of bravery daily, so that larger storms feel like the next size up of what you already know.

Seneca urged: *"Let us prepare our minds as if we'd come to the very end of life... let us balance life's account every day."*

Balance it tonight—not with grand gestures, but with the next clean act: say what is true and kind, do what is right and brave, lay down what is not yours to carry. Sleep as one who may leave life at any moment, and therefore knows how to live it.

This is your tenth reset: to face the future with courage. Not by chasing certainty, but by training clarity, acceptance, and strength for whatever emerges through the mist.

Epilogue
The Calm Within You

Why steadiness is a journey, not a destination

The Pocket Compass (a parable)

On the morning she thought she might quit, she walked to the end of the pier. Wind lifted the water in small white fists; gulls wrote their arguments across the gray. She had packed a notebook, a pen, and the conviction that she needed a map—something comprehensive and final, a diagram that would keep days from knocking her sideways.

An older man in a knit cap was mending nets nearby.

"Storm?" he asked, glancing at the sky.

"Inside," she said, tapping her chest. "I keep losing my way. I want a map that won't change."

He touched the pocket of his jacket and pulled out a simple compass. The brass was scuffed; the needle hardly rested.

"Maps go stale," he said. "Tides, sandbars, politics. But a compass—if you check it—stays honest. It won't steer the boat for you. It will just keep pointing while you row."

He pressed it into her palm. "Use this, and start where you are. Check often. Correct gently. That's how you cross water that doesn't keep still."

The pier didn't quiet. The wind stayed. She didn't get a map that solved her life. She walked home with a compass, and, to her surprise, that was better.

This book has been a way of handing you such a compass. Not a grand design; a reliable point. Not the promise of calm weather; the practice of a calm hand.

A Reset as an Ongoing Journey

If you came here looking for a final page where everything locks into place—where storms vanish, the emails stop, and every driver uses a turn signal—you won't find it. Calm is not a prize you win. It is a discipline you keep.

The resets in these chapters were not boxes to check off but tools to return to. Some days you will forget. Some days you will drift. But each return is progress. That is why the compass metaphor works: not because it gives you a route, but because it keeps you oriented no matter how many times you stray.

The Stoics knew this. Marcus Aurelius wrote his reminders daily, not once. Epictetus repeated simple distinctions until they were second nature. Seneca counseled his friends again and again to pause, reflect, and act cleanly. They did not imagine a graduation from practice. They saw practice itself as life.

Your resets will function the same way. Some mornings you will begin with intention. Other mornings you'll rush into noise and only remember at noon. Both are part of the craft. Calm is not about perfection; it's about returning—checking the compass, correcting, and moving on.

Why Small, Consistent Actions Shape Character

We often imagine change as dramatic: thunderclaps of inspiration, sudden turning points. More often, transformation sounds like the quiet tick of a metronome—steady, ordinary, stubborn.

Marcus Aurelius observed that character is "dyed with the color of your thoughts." Dye doesn't set in a single dip; it takes repetition. The vat deepens only by returning the cloth again and again.

The same is true for your resets:

- Choosing perspective instead of panic.
- Dropping a grudge instead of rehearsing it.
- Saying "enough" instead of chasing more.
- Returning to a breath when anger climbs your throat.

None of these are spectacular. None will trend online. Yet they accumulate. Rehearsals become habits; habits become character. By the time others notice and call you "calm," it won't be because storms stopped coming. It will be because you stopped fighting winds you cannot command and started steering with the ones you can.

Consistency may look boring, but it builds bridges—strong, invisible, and steady enough for others to cross.

Calm and the Virtues Revisited

In Reset 5, you anchored yourself in values: wisdom, justice, courage, self-control. In Reset 8, you learned to protect calm through rhythm. Here, at the close, those threads braid together.

Calm is not the highest Stoic good—virtue is. But calm is the soil that makes virtue possible. Without calm, wisdom is drowned in panic. Without calm, courage becomes rashness. Without calm, justice warps under anger. Without calm, self-control cracks at the first provocation.

When you practice calm, you are not aiming at passivity. You are creating space for your better self to choose. You are giving virtue room to breathe. You are choosing posture over panic.

The Cost of Restlessness

Restlessness is not neutral. It corrodes focus, making each task slower. It erodes relationships, because distraction feels like absence. It burns through energy, because constant reaction leaves no margin for recovery.

Over time, restlessness seeps into identity. Each time you lash out in frustration or spiral in comparison, you carve a groove. Grooves become habits. Habits shape character. Without noticing, you become what you repeatedly rehearse.

But calm works the same way in reverse. Each time you pause, breathe, and act deliberately, you carve a groove toward steadiness. Each time you drop a grudge or resist a reflex, you build character. Calm rehearsed becomes calm lived.

The Compass as Lifelong Practice

The compass you now carry is not meant to sit unused. Its gift is orientation. But orientation requires attention.

Three ways to keep checking it:

1. **Pause often.** When overwhelmed, stop and ask: *What is mine to do?* That is the compass line.

2. **Correct gently.** No sailor curses the needle for drifting; they adjust. Self-correction works the same way.

3. **Return daily.** Morning intention, mid-day reset, evening reflection—each is a compass-check. Each is a chance to realign.

Maps grow stale. The future will not give you a master plan. But the compass remains faithful. And the compass you hold is nothing more than your ability to pause, to choose, to act in alignment with your values.

An Invitation to Live Steady, Calm, and Unshaken

As you leave these pages, you do not leave Stoicism. You carry it—light but steady—like the compass in your pocket. Use it when the fog rolls in, when the voices grow loud, when the sea grows rough.

You are not asked to become someone else. You are asked to become the person you meant when you were quiet.

Live steady. Lower your center of gravity with simple rituals. Put your phone in another room sometimes. Eat one meal with your eyes and tongue, not a screen. Walk when you could scroll.

Live calm. Not as the absence of feeling, but as the refusal to be driven by first feelings alone. Calm is not slowness; it is deliberateness. Calm can move fast when needed, slow when haste is vanity.

Live unshaken. Not because nothing touches you, but because what touches you meets a person with a spine. You will grieve. You will be wrong and wronged. To be unshaken is to continue—repairing what you can, protecting what you must, and laying down what you cannot carry without breaking something better.

A Small Vow

If you want a vow small enough to carry in your breath, let it be this:

- I will do what is mine, ask for what I need, and let the rest be.
- I will be clear and kind.
- I will begin again quickly and without drama.

If you want a measure, choose one that lives in your power:

- Did I keep my word?
- Did I treat others fairly?
- Did I practice courage when fear chirped?
- Did I steer my attention where it can do good?

If you want companions, walk with those who don't confuse volume with value, who give credit forward, who apologize without speeches, and forgive without crowns. Let your steadiness amplify theirs.

The Calm Within

You may not control the waters. You may not control the weather. But you can row with clarity, courage, and calm. Again and again. That is enough.

The compass in your pocket is not perfection. It is practice. When the world shakes, check your compass. Correct gently. Then keep rowing. Calm is not ahead of you. Calm is already within you.

Request for a Review

Dear Reader,

Thank you for reading *The Calm Within: A Stoic Reset to Reclaim Your Inner Power*. I hope these pages have offered you calm, courage, and a steady compass for your journey.

If the book has been meaningful to you, I would be grateful if you could take a moment to leave a review. Reviews help other readers discover the book and decide if it's right for them.

If you purchased the book on **Amazon**, you can leave your review here: ☞ **https://amzn.to/4pHa54V**

Or scan here to leave your Amazon review:

If you purchased it through **another store**, I encourage you to share your feedback directly on that platform.

Your words make a real difference — not only to me as an author, but also to readers who may be looking for the same guidance you found.

With gratitude,

Rodolfo Costa

About the Author

Rodolfo Costa is an author whose work explores how ancient wisdom can guide us through the pressures of modern life. With a deep passion for Stoic philosophy and personal growth, his writing centers on Stoicism, mindfulness, and practical philosophy—always with the aim of making timeless insights accessible and actionable for everyday readers.

His works — *Stoic Kids: 44 Stories That Teach Calm, Courage, and Character*, *The Stoic Path: Finding Meaning, Virtue, and Serenity in Everyday Life*, and *The Stoic Prompt Journal: Cultivate Resilience, Wisdom, and Inner Peace* — form a body of work devoted to resilience, clarity, and inner strength. Together, these books have established him as a guiding voice for readers seeking calm and courage in a turbulent world.

As a business owner, former Realtor, and lifelong student, Costa blends timeless wisdom with practical insights from everyday life. His purpose is steady: to help readers find calm not as escape, but as discipline—meeting life with clarity, courage, and self-control.

Living in Northern California, he continues to study and apply Stoic principles, inspiring others to pursue their own path of growth.

www.ingramcontent.com/pod-product-compliance
Lightning Source LLC
Chambersburg PA
CBHW020942090426
42736CB00010B/1229